CLASSIC POEMS FOR
MOTHERS

CLASSIC POEMS FOR MOTHERS

Summersdale Publishers Ltd
46 West Street
Chichester
West Sussex
PO19 1RP
UK

www.summersdale.com

Printed and bound in China

ISBN: 978-1-84953-210-5

Substantial discounts on bulk quantities of Summersdale books are available to corporations, professional associations and other organisations. For details contact Summersdale Publishers by telephone (+44-1243-771107), fax (+44-1243-786300) or email (nicky@summersdale.com).

CLASSIC POEMS FOR
MOTHERS

COMPILED BY MAX MORRIS

summersdale

CONTENTS

THE MOTHER MOON

The moon upon the wide sea
Placidly looks down,
Smiling with her mild face,
Though the ocean frown.
Clouds may dim her brightness,
But soon they pass away,
And she shines out, unaltered,
O'er the little waves at play.
So 'mid the storm or sunshine,
Wherever she may go,
Led on by her hidden power
The wild see must plow.

As the tranquil evening moon
Looks on that restless sea,
So a mother's gentle face,
Little child, is watching thee.
Then banish every tempest,
Chase all your clouds away,
That smoothly and brightly

Your quiet heart may play.
Let cheerful looks and actions
Like shining ripples flow,
Following the mother's voice,
Singing as they go.

Louisa May Alcott

FROM ROCK ME TO SLEEP

Backward, turn backward, O Time, in your flight,
Make me a child again just for to-night!
Mother, come back from the echoless shore,
Take me again to your heart as of yore;
Kiss from my forehead the furrows of care,
Smooth the few silver threads out of my hair;
Over my slumbers your loving watch keep; –
Rock me to sleep, mother, – rock me to sleep!

Backward, flow backward, O tide of the years!
I am so weary of toil and of tears, –
Toil without recompense, tears all in vain, –
Take them, and give me my childhood again!
I have grown weary of dust and decay, –
Weary of flinging my soul-wealth away;
Weary of sowing for others to reap; –
Rock me to sleep, mother, – rock me to sleep!

Elizabeth Akers Allen

AMY MARGARET'S FIVE YEARS OLD

Amy Margaret's five years old,
Amy Margaret's hair is gold,
Dearer twenty-thousand-fold
Than gold, is Amy Margaret.
'Amy' is friend, is 'Margaret'
The pearl for crown or carkanet?
Or peeping daisy, summer's pet?
Which are you, Amy Margaret?
A friend, a daisy, and a pearl,
A kindly, simple, precious girl, –
Such, howsoe'er the world may twirl,
Be ever, – Amy Margaret!

William Allingham

A SEED

See how a Seed, which Autumn flung down,
And through the Winter neglected lay,
Uncoils two little green leaves and two brown,
With tiny root taking hold on the clay
As, lifting and strengthening day by day,
It pushes red branchless, sprouts new leaves,
And cell after cell the Power in it weaves
Out of the storehouse of soil and clime,
To fashion a Tree in due course of time;
Tree with rough bark and boughs' expansion,
Where the Crow can build his mansion,
Or a Man, in some new May,
Lie under whispering leaves and say,
'Are the ills of one's life so very bad
When a Green Tree makes me deliciously glad?'
As I do now. But where shall I be
When this little Seed is a tall green Tree?

William Allingham

THERE IS A LADY SWEET AND KIND

There is a Lady sweet and kind,
Was never face so pleased my mind;
I did but see her passing by,
And yet I love her till I die.

Her gesture, motion, and her smiles,
Her wit, her voice my heart beguiles,
Beguiles my heart, I know not why,
And yet I love her till I die.

Cupid is wingèd and doth range,
Her country so my love doth change:
But change she earth, or change she sky,
Yet will I love her till I die.

Anonymous

FROM A MOTHER TO HER WAKING INFANT

Thy smooth round cheek so soft and warm;
Thy pinky hand and dimpled arm;
Thy silken locks that scantly peep,
With gold-tipp'd ends, where circles deep,
Around thy neck in harmless grace
So soft and sleekly hold their place,
Might harder hearts with kindness fill,
And gain our right good will.

Each passing clown bestows his blessing,
Thy mouth is worn with old wives' kissing:
E'en lighter looks the gloomy eye
Of surly sense when thou art by;
And yet, I think, whoe'er they be,
They love thee not like me.

Perhaps when time shall add a few
Short months to thee, thou'lt love me too;
And after that, through life's long way.
Become my sure and cheering stay:
Wilt care for me and be my hold,
When I am weak and old.

Thou'lt listen to my lengthen'd tale,
And pity me when I am frail –
But see! the sweepy swimming fly,
Upon the window takes thine eye.
Go to thy little senseless play;
Thou dost not heed my lay.

Joanna Baillie

MOTHER'S EVENING PRAYER

O gentle presence, peace and joy and power;
O Life divine, that owns each waiting hour,
Thou Love that guards the nestling's faltering flight!
Keep Thou my child on upward wing tonight.

Love is our refuge; only with mine eye
Can I behold the snare, the pit, the fall:
His habitation high is here, and nigh,
His arm encircles me, and mine, and all.

O make me glad for every scalding tear,
For hope deferred, ingratitude, disdain!
Wait, and love more for every hate, and fear
No ill, – since God is good, and loss is gain.

Beneath the shadow of His mighty wing;
In that sweet secret of the narrow way,
Seeking and finding, with the angels sing:
'Lo, I am with you alway,' – watch and pray.

No snare, no fowler, pestilence or pain;
No night drops down upon the troubled breast,
When heaven's aftersmile earth's tear-drops gain,
And mother finds her home and heav'nly rest.

Mary Baker Eddy

A CHILD'S THOUGHT OF GOD

They say that God lives very high;
But if you look above the pines
You can not see our God; and why?

And if you dig down in the mines,
You never see him in the gold;
Though from him all that's glory shines.

God is so good, he wears a fold
Of heaven and earth across his face –
Like secrets kept for love untold.

But still I feel that his embrace
Slides down by thrills through all things made,
Through sight and sound of every place.

As if my tender mother laid
On my shut lips her kisses' pressure,
Half waking me at night, and said,
'Who kissed you through the dark, dear guesser?'

Elizabeth Barrett Browning

INFANT SORROW

My mother groaned, my father wept,
Into the dangerous world I leapt;
Helpless, naked, piping loud,
Like a fiend hid in a cloud.

Struggling in my father's hands,
Striving against my swaddling bands,
Bound and weary, I thought best
To sulk upon my mother's breast.

William Blake

A CRADLE SONG

Sleep, sleep, beauty bright,
Dreaming in the joys of night;
Sleep, sleep; in thy sleep
Little sorrows sit and weep.

Sweet babe, in thy face
Soft desires I can trace,
Secret joys and secret smiles,
Little pretty infant wiles.

As thy softest limbs I feel
Smiles as of the morning steal
O'er thy cheek, and o'er thy breast
Where thy little heart doth rest.

O the cunning wiles that creep
In thy little heart asleep!
When thy little heart doth wake,
Then the dreadful night shall break.

William Blake

REEDS OF INNOCENCE

Piping down the valleys wild,
Piping songs of pleasant glee,
On a cloud I saw a child,
And he laughing said to me:

'Pipe a song about a Lamb!'
So I piped with merry cheer.
'Piper, pipe that song again;'
So I piped: he wept to hear.

'Drop thy pipe, thy happy pipe;
Sing thy songs of happy cheer!'
So I sung the same again,
While he wept with joy to hear.

'Piper, sit thee down and write
In a book that all may read.'
So he vanish'd from my sight;
And I pluck'd a hollow reed,

And I made a rural pen,
And I stain'd the water clear,
And I wrote my happy songs
Every child may joy to hear.

William Blake

TO MY DEAR CHILDREN

This Book by Any yet unread,
I leave for you when I am dead,
That, being gone, here you may find
What was your liveing mother's mind.
Make use of what I leave in Love
And God shall blesse you from above.

Anne Bradstreet

MY DELIGHT AND THY DELIGHT

My delight and thy delight
Walking, like two angels white,
In the gardens of the night:

My desire and thy desire
Twining to a tongue of fire,
Leaping live, and laughing higher:

Thro' the everlasting strife
In the mystery of life.
Love, from whom the world begun,
Hath the secret of the sun.

Love can tell, and love alone,
Whence the million stars were strewn,
Why each atom knows its own,
How, in spite of woe and death,
Gay is life, and sweet is breath:

This he taught us, this we knew,

Happy in his science true,

Hand in hand as we stood

'Neath the shadows of the wood,

Heart to heart as we lay

In the dawning of the day.

Robert Bridges

BROTHER AND SISTER

'Sister, sister, go to bed!
Go and rest your weary head.'
Thus the prudent brother said.

'Do you want a battered hide,
Or scratches to your face applied?'
Thus his sister calm replied.

'Sister, do not raise my wrath.
I'd make you into mutton broth
As easily as kill a moth.'

The sister raised her beaming eye
And looked on him indignantly
And sternly answered, 'Only try!'

Off to the cook he quickly ran.
'Dear Cook, please lend a frying-pan
To me as quickly as you can.'

'And wherefore should I lend it you?'
'The reason, Cook, is plain to view.
I wish to make an Irish stew.'

'What meat is in that stew to go?'
'My sister'll be the contents!'
'Oh'
'You'll lend the pan to me, Cook?'
'No!'

Moral: Never stew your sister.

Lewis Carroll

A NURSERY DARLING

A Mother's breast:
Safe refuge from her childish fears,
From childish troubles, childish tears,
Mists that enshroud her dawning years!
see how in sleep she seems to sing
A voiceless psalm – an offering
Raised, to the glory of her King
In Love: for Love is Rest.

A Darling's kiss:
Dearest of all the signs that fleet
From lips that lovingly repeat
Again, again, the message sweet!
Full to the brim with girlish glee,
A child, a very child is she,
Whose dream of heaven is still to be
At Home: for Home is Bliss.

Lewis Carroll

WHEN LOVELY WOMAN

When lovely woman wants a favor,
And finds, too late, that man won't bend,
What earthly circumstance can save her
From disappointment in the end?

The only way to bring him over
The last experiment to try,
Whether a husband or a lover,
If he have feeling, is, to cry!

Phoebe Cary

AFFECTION

The earth that made the rose,
She also is thy mother, and not I.
The flame wherewith thy maiden spirit glows
Was lighted at no hearth that I sit by.
I am as far below as heaven above thee.
Were I thine angel, more I could not love thee.

Bid me defend thee!
Thy danger over-human strength shall lend me,
A hand of iron and a heart of steel,
To strike, to wound, to slay, and not to feel.
But if you chide me,
I am a weak, defenceless child beside thee.

Mary Elizabeth Coleridge

ANSWER TO A CHILD'S QUESTION

Do you ask what the birds say? The Sparrow, the Dove,

The Linnet and Thrush say, 'I love and I love!'

In the winter they're silent – the wind is so strong;

What it says, I don't know, but it sings a loud song.

But green leaves, and blossoms, and sunny warm weather,

And singing, and loving – all come back together.

But the Lark is so brimful of gladness and love,

The green fields below him, the blue sky above,

That he sings, and he sings; and for ever sings he –

'I love my Love, and my Love loves me!'

Samuel Taylor Coleridge

THE CHILD

See yon blithe child that dances in our sight!
Can gloomy shadows fall from one so bright?
Fond mother, whence these fears?
While buoyantly he rushes o'er the lawn,
Dream not of clouds to stain his manhood's dawn,
Nor dim that sight with tears.

No cloud he spies in brightly glowing hours,
But feels as if the newly vested bowers
For him could never fade:
Too well we know that vernal pleasures fleet,
But having him, so gladsome, fair, and sweet,
Our loss is overpaid.

Amid the balmiest flowers that earth can give
Some bitter drops distil, and all that live
A mingled portion share;
But, while he learns these truths which we lament,
Such fortitude as ours will sure be sent,
Such solace to his care.

Sara Coleridge

A MARRIAGE RING

The ring, so worn as you behold,
So thin, so pale, is yet of gold:
The passion such it was to prove –
Worn with life's care, love yet was love.

George Crabbe

THE MOTHER BIRD

Through the green twilight of a hedge
I peered, with cheek on the cool leaves pressed,
And spied a bird upon a nest:
Two eyes she had beseeching me
Meekly and brave, and her brown breast
Throbbed hot and quick above her heart;
And then she opened her dagger bill, –
'Twas not a chirp, as sparrows pipe
At break of day; 'twas not a trill,
As falters through the quiet even;
But one sharp solitary note,
One desperate, fierce, and vivid cry
Of valiant tears, and hopeless joy,
One passionate note of victory;
Off, like a fool afraid, I sneaked,
Smiling the smile the fool smiles best,
At the mother bird in the secret hedge
Patient upon her lonely nest.

Walter de la Mare

FROM THE CHILDREN

When the lessons and tasks are all ended,
And the school for the day is dismissed,
And the little ones gather around me,
To bid me good-night and be kissed;
Oh, the little white arms that encircle
My neck in a tender embrace!
Oh, the smiles that are haloes of heaven,
Shedding sunshine of love on my face!

Charles M. Dickinson

BLISS IS THE PLAYTHING OF THE CHILD

Bliss is the plaything of the child –
The secret of the man
The sacred stealth of Boy and Girl
Rebuke it if we can.

Emily Dickinson

NATURE, THE GENTLEST MOTHER

Nature, the gentlest mother
Impatient of no child,
The feeblest or the waywardest –
Her admonition mild

In forest and the hill
By traveller is heard,
Restraining rampant squirrel
Or too impetuous bird.

How fair her conversation
A summer afternoon –
Her household, her assembly;
And when the sun goes down

Her voice among the aisles
Incite the timid prayer
Of the minutest cricket,
The most unworthy flower.

When all the children sleep
She turns as long away
As will suffice to light her lamps;
Then, bending from the sky,

With infinite affection
And infiniter care,
Her golden finger on her lip,
Wills silence everywhere.

Emily Dickinson

IF NATURE SMILES –
THE MOTHER MUST

If Nature smiles – the Mother must

I'm sure, at many a whim

Of Her eccentric Family –

Is She so much to blame?

Emily Dickinson

A CHILD IN THE GARDEN

When to the garden of untroubled thought
I came of late, and saw the open door,
And wished again to enter, and explore
The sweet, wild ways with stainless bloom inwrought,
And bowers of innocence with beauty fraught,
It seemed some purer voice must speak before
I dared to tread that garden loved of yore,
That Eden lost unknown and found unsought.

Then just within the gate I saw a child, –
A stranger-child, yet to my heart most dear;
He held his hands to me, and softly smiled
With eyes that knew no shade of sin or fear:
'Come in,' he said, 'and play awhile with me;'
'I am the little child you used to be.'

Henry van Dyke

A HOME SONG

I read within a poet's book
A word that starred the page:
'Stone walls do not a prison make,
Nor iron bars a cage!'

Yes, that is true; and something more
You'll find, where'er you roam,
That marble floors and gilded walls
Can never make a home.

But every house where Love abides,
And Friendship is a guest,
Is surely home, and home-sweet-home:
For there the heart can rest.

Henry van Dyke

A PRAYER FOR
A MOTHER'S BIRTHDAY

Lord Jesus, Thou hast known

A mother's love and tender care:

And Thou wilt hear, while for my own

Mother most dear I make this birthday prayer.

Protect her life, I pray,

Who gave the gift of life to me;

And may she know, from day to day,

The deepening glow of Life that comes from Thee.

As once upon her breast

Fearless and well content I lay,

So let her heart, on Thee at rest,

Feel fears depart and troubles fade away.

Her every wish fulfill;

And even if Thou must refuse

In anything, let Thy wise will

A comfort bring such as kind mothers use.

Ah, hold her by the hand,
As once her hand held mine;
And though she may not understand
Life's winding way, lead her in peace divine.

I cannot pay my debt
For all the love that she has given;
But Thou, love's Lord, wilt not forget
Her due reward, – bless her in earth and heaven.

Henry van Dyke

FROM BROTHER AND SISTER

I.

I cannot choose but think upon the time
When our two lives grew like two buds that kiss
At lightest thrill from the bee's swinging chime,
Because the one so near the other is.

He was the elder and a little man
Of forty inches, bound to show no dread,
And I the girl that puppy-like now ran,
Now lagged behind my brother's larger tread.

I held him wise, and when he talked to me
Of snakes and birds, and which God loved the best,
I thought his knowledge marked the boundary
Where men grew blind, though angels knew the rest.

If he said 'Hush!' I tried to hold my breath;
Wherever he said 'Come!' I stepped in faith.

II.

Long years have left their writing on my brow,
But yet the freshness and the dew-fed beam
Of those young mornings are about me now,
When we two wandered toward the far-off stream

With rod and line. Our basket held a store
Baked for us only, and I thought with joy
That I should have my share, though he had more,
Because he was the elder and a boy.

The firmaments of daisies since to me
Have had those mornings in their opening eyes,
The bunchèd cowslip's pale transparency
Carries that sunshine of sweet memories,

And wild-rose branches take their finest scent
From those blest hours of infantine content.

George Eliot

CHILD AND MOTHER

O mother-my-love, if you'll give me your hand,
And go where I ask you to wander,
I will lead you away to a beautiful land, –
The Dreamland that's waiting out yonder.
We'll walk in a sweet posie-garden out there,
Where moonlight and starlight are streaming,
And the flowers and the birds are filling the air
With the fragrance and music of dreaming.

There'll be no little tired-out boy to undress,
No questions or cares to perplex you,
There'll be no little bruises or bumps to caress,
Nor patching of stockings to vex you;
For I'll rock you away on a silver-dew stream
And sing you asleep when you're weary,
And no one shall know of our beautiful dream
But you and your own little dearie.

And when I am tired I'll nestle my head
In the bosom that's soothed me so often,

And the wide-awake stars shall sing, in my stead,

A song which our dreaming shall soften.

So, Mother-my-Love, let me take your dear hand,

And away through the starlight we'll wander, –

Away through the mist to the beautiful land, –

The Dreamland that's waiting out yonder.

Eugene Field

A LETTER TO DAPHNIS

This is to the crown and blessing of my life,
The much loved husband of a happy wife;
To him whose constant passion found the art
To win a stubborn and ungrateful heart,
And to the world by tenderest proof discovers
They err, who say that husbands can't be lovers.
With such return of passion as is due,
Daphnis I love, Daphnis my thoughts pursue;
Daphnis, my hopes and joys are bounded all in you.
Even I, for Daphnis' and my promise' sake,
What I in woman censure, undertake.
But this from love, not vanity, proceeds;
You know who writes, and I who 'tis that reads.
Judge not my passion by my want of skill:
Many love well, though they express it ill;
And I your censure could with pleasure bear,
Would you but soon return, and speak it here.

Anne Finch

BABY

Dimpled and flushed and dewy pink he lies,

Crumpled and tossed and lapt in snowy bands;

Aimlessly reaching with his tiny hands,

Lifting in wondering gaze his great blue eyes.

Sweet pouting lips, parted by breathing sighs;

Soft cheeks, warm-tinted as from tropic lands;

Framed with brown hair in shining silken strands, –

All fair, all pure, a sunbeam from the skies!

O perfect innocence! O soul enshrined

In blissful ignorance of good or ill,

By never gale of idle passion crossed!

Although thou art no alien from thy kind,

Though pain and death may take thee captive, still

Through sin, at least, thine Eden is not lost.

Elaine Goodale Eastman

FROM THE ADOPTED CHILD

'Oh! green is the turf where my brothers play,
Through the long bright hours of the summer day;
They find the red cup-moss where they climb,
And they chase the bee o'er the scented thyme,
And the rocks where the heath-flower blooms they know –
Lady, kind lady! O, let me go!'

'Content thee, boy! in my bower to dwell.
Here are sweet sounds which thou lovest well;
Flutes on the air in the stilly noon,
Harps which the wandering breezes tune,
And the silvery wood-note of many a bird
Whose voice was ne'er in thy mountains heard.'

'Oh! my mother sings, at the twilight's fall,
A song of the hills far more sweet than all;
She sings it under our own green tree
To the babe half slumbering on her knee;
I dreamt last night of that music low –
Lady, kind lady! O, let me go!'

Felicia Dorothea Hemans

A CHILD'S GRACE

Here a little child I stand
Heaving up my either hand;
Cold as paddocks though they be,
Here I lift them up to Thee,
For a benison to fall
On our meat and on us all. Amen.

Robert Herrick

A BOY'S SONG

Where the pools are bright and deep,
Where the grey trout lies asleep,
Up the river and over the lea,
That's the way for Billy and me.

Where the blackbird sings the latest,
Where the hawthorn blooms the sweetest,
Where the nestlings chirp and flee,
That's the way for Billy and me.

Where the mowers mow the cleanest,
Where the hay lies thick and greenest,
There to track the homeward bee,
That's the way for Billy and me.

Where the hazel bank is steepest,
Where the shadow falls the deepest,
Where the clustering nuts fall free,
That's the way for Billy and me.

Why the boys should drive away
Little sweet maidens from the play,
Or love to banter and fight so well,
That's the thing I never could tell.

But this I know, I love to play
Through the meadow, among the hay;
Up the water and over the lea,
That's the way for Billy and me.

James Hogg

TO A CHILD EMBRACING HIS MOTHER

Love thy mother, little one!
Kiss and clasp her neck again, –
Hereafter she may have a son
Will kiss and clasp her neck in vain.
Love thy mother, little one!

Gaze upon her living eyes,
And mirror back her love for thee, –
Hereafter thou mayst shudder sighs
To meet them when they cannot see.
Gaze upon her living eyes!

Press her lips the while they glow
With love that they have often told, –
Hereafter thou mayst press in woe,
And kiss them till thine own are cold.
Press her lips the while they glow!

Oh, revere her raven hair!
Although it be not silver-gray;
Too early death, led on by Care,
May snatch save one dear lock away.
Oh, revere her raven hair!

Pray for her at eve and morn,
That heaven may long the stroke defer, –
For thou mayst live the hour forlorn
When thou wilt ask to die with her.
Pray for her at eve and morn!

Thomas Hood

THE MEANS TO ATTAIN HAPPY LIFE

Martial, the things that do attain
The happy life be these, I find: –
The richesse left, not got with pain;
The fruitful ground, the quiet mind;

The equal friend; no grudge, no strife;
No charge of rule, nor governance;
Without disease, the healthful life;
The household of continuance;

The mean diet, no delicate fare;
True wisdom join'd with simpleness;
The night dischargèd of all care,
Where wine the wit may not oppress.

The faithful wife, without debate;
Such sleeps as may beguile the night:
Contented with thine own estate
Ne wish for death, ne fear his might.

Henry Howard, Earl of Surrey

MY MOTHER BIDS ME BIND MY HAIR

My mother bids me bind my hair,
With bands of rosy hue,
Tie up my sleeves with ribbons rare,
And lace my bodice blue.

'For why', she cries, 'sit still and weep,
While others dance and play?'
Alas! I scarce can go or creep
While Lubin is away.

'Tis sad to think the days are gone
When those we love were near;
I sit upon this mossy stone
And sigh when none can hear.

And while I spin my flaxen thread,
And sing my simple lay,
The village seems asleep or dead,
Now Lubin is away.

Anne Hunter

MOTHER AND SON

Postman, good postman, halt I pray,
And leave a letter for me to-day;
If it's only a line from over the sea
To say that my Sandy remembers me.

I have waited and hoped by day and by night;
I'll watch – if spared – till my locks grow white;
Have prayed – yet repent that my faith waxed dim,
When passing, you left no message from him.

My proud arms cradled his infant head,
My prayers arose by his boyhood's bed;
To better our fortunes, he traversed the main;
God guard him, and bring him to me again.

The postman has passed midst the beating rain,
And my heart is bowed with its weight of pain;
This dark, dark day, I am tortured with dread
That Sandy, my boy, may be ill or dead.

But hark! there's a step! my heart be still!
A step at the gate, in the path, on the sill;
Did the postman return? my letter forget?
Oh 'tis Sandy! Thank God, he loves me yet!

Mary Eliza Ireland

TO MY MOTHER

Gentlest of critics, does your memory hold
(I know it does) a record of the days
When I, a schoolboy, earned your generous praise
For halting verse and stories crudely told?
Over these childish scrawls the years have rolled,
They might not know the world's unfriendly gaze;
But still your smile shines down familiar ways,
Touches my words and turns their dross to gold.

More dear to-day than in that vanished time
Comes your nigh praise to make me proud and strong.
In my poor notes you hear Love's splendid chime,
So unto you does this, my work belong.
Take, then, a little gift of fragile rhyme:
Your heart will change it to authentic song.

Joyce Kilmer

MOTHER O' MINE

If I were hanged on the highest hill,
Mother o' mine, O mother o' mine!
I know whose love would follow me still,
Mother o' mine, O mother o' mine!

If I were drowned in the deepest sea,
Mother o' mine, O mother o' mine!
I know whose tears would come down to me,
Mother o' mine, O mother o' mine!

If I were damned of body and soul,
I know whose prayers would make me whole,
Mother o' mine, O mother o' mine!

Rudyard Kipling

THE MOTHER'S HOPE

Is there, when the winds are singing
In the happy summer time, –
When the raptured air is ringing
With Earth's music heavenward springing

Forest chirp, and village chime, –
Is there, of the sounds that float
Unsighingly, a single note
Half so sweet, and clear, and wild,
As the laughter of a child?

Listen! and be now delighted:
Morn hath touched her golden strings;
Earth and Sky their vows have plighted;
Life and Light are reunited

Amid countless carollings;
Yet, delicious as they are,
There's a sound that's sweeter far, -
One that makes the heart rejoice
More than all, – the human voice!

Organ finer, deeper, clearer,
Though it be a stranger's tone, –
Than the winds or waters dearer,
More enchanting to the hearer,

For it answereth to his own.
But, of all its witching words,
Those are sweetest, bubbling wild
Through the laugher of a child.

Harmonies from time-touched towers,
Haunted strains from rivulets,
Hum of bees among the flowers,
Rustling leaves, and silver showers, –

These, erelong, the ear forgets;
But in mine there is a sound
Ringing on the whole year round, –
Heart-deep laughter that I heard
Ere my child could speak a word.

Ah! 'twas heard by ear far purer,
Fondlier formed to catch the strain, –

Ear of one whose love is surer, –
Hers, the mother, the endurer

Of the deepest share of pain;
Here the deepest bliss to treasure
Memories of that cry of peasure;
Hers to hoard, a lifetime after,
Echoes of that infant laughter.

'Tis a mother's large affection
Hears with a mysterious sense, –
Breathings that evade detection,
Whisper faint, and fine inflection,

Thrill in her with power intense.
Chidhood's honeyed words untaught
Hiveth she in loving thought, –
Tones that never thence depart;
For she listens – with her heart.

Samuel Laman Blanchard

A CHILD

A child's a plaything for an hour;
Its pretty tricks we try
For that or for a longer space –
Then tire, and lay it by.

But I knew one that to itself
All seasons could control;
That would have mock'd the sense of pain
Out of a grieved soul.

Thou straggler into loving arms,
Young climber-up of knees,
When I forget thy thousand ways
Then life and all shall cease.

Mary Lamb

A BABY ASLEEP AFTER PAIN

As a drenched, drowned bee

Hangs numb and heavy from a bending flower,

So clings to me

My baby, her brown hair brushed with wet tears

And laid against her cheek;

Her soft white legs hanging heavily over my arm

Swinging heavily to my movements as I walk.

My sleeping baby hangs upon my life,

Like a burden she hangs on me.

She has always seemed so light,

But now she is wet with tears and numb with pain

Even her floating hair sinks heavily,

Reaching downwards;

As the wings of a drenched, drowned bee

Are a heaviness, and a weariness.

David Herbert Lawrence

A BABY RUNNING BAREFOOT

When the bare feet of the baby beat across the grass
The little white feet nod like white flowers in the wind,
They poise and run like ripples lapping across the water;
And the sight of their white play among the grass
Is like a little robin's song, winsome,
Or as two white butterflies settle in the cup of one flower
For a moment, then away with a flutter of wings.

I long for the baby to wander hither to me
Like a wind-shadow wandering over the water,
So that she can stand on my knee
With her little bare feet in my hands,
Cool like syringa buds,
Firm and silken like pink young peony flowers.

David Herbert Lawrence

MY MOTHER

God made my mother on an April day,
From sorrow and the mist along the sea,
Lost birds' and wanderers' songs and ocean spray,
And the moon loved her wandering jealously.

Beside the ocean's din she combed her hair,
Singing the nocturne of the passing ships,
Before her earthly lover found her there
And kissed away the music from her lips.

She came unto the hills and saw the change
That brings the swallow and the geese in turns.
But there was not a grief she deeméd strange,
For there is that in her which always mourns.

Kind heart she has for all on hill or wave
Whose hopes grew wings like ants to fly away.
I bless the God Who such a mother gave
This poor bird-hearted singer of a day.

Francis Ledwidge

NATURE

As a fond mother, when the day is o'er,

Leads by the hand her little child to bed,

Half willing, half reluctant to be led,

And leave his broken playthings on the floor,

Still gazing at them through the open door,

Nor wholly reassured and comforted

By promises of others in their stead,

Which, though more splendid, may not please him more;

So Nature deals with us, and takes away

Our playthings one by one, and by the hand

Leads us to rest so gently, that we go

Scarce knowing if we wished to go or stay,

Being too full of sleep to understand

How far the unknown transcends the what we know.

Henry Wadsworth Longfellow

TO A CHILD

I love to look on that eye of blue,
For tears have not yet worn a channel through;
And the few bright summers since thy birth,
Have left thee a stranger still on earth.

A stranger – and all, to thine untaught eyes,
Is bright with the hues of paradise.
The rapture of being thrills thy frame,
And sorrow thou know'st not even by name.

Thy innocent thoughts, unswayed by art,
Gush from the depths of thy guileless heart;
Like a harp when the wandering breezes sigh,
Answering each touch with melody.

I would, sweet one, I might wish for thee,
That a stranger thus thou shouldst ever be;
That time might not lift the enchanted veil,
Nor breathe in thine ear his mournful tale.

But those who are bid to this feast of life,
Must drink the cup, – must abide the strife: –
Then it were better to wish for thee,
Strength for the conflict, and victory.

Anne Lynch Botta

BABY

Where did you come from, baby dear?
Out of the everywhere into the here.

Where did you get your eyes so blue?
Out of the sky as I came through.

What makes the light in them sparkle and spin?
Some of the starry spikes left in.

Where did you get that little tear?
I found it waiting when I got here.

What makes your forehead so smooth and high?
A soft hand stroked it as I went by.

What makes your cheek like a warm white rose?
Something better than any one knows.

Whence that three-cornered smile of bliss?
Three angels gave me at once a kiss.

Where did you get that pearly ear?
God spoke, and it came out to hear.

Where did you get those arms and hands?
Love made itself into hooks and bands.

Feet, whence did you come, you darling things?
From the same box as the cherub's wings.

How did they all just come to be you?
God thought about me, and so I grew.

But how did you come to us, you dear?
God thought of *you,* and so I am here.

George MacDonald

BEDTIME

'Come, children, put away your toys;
Roll up the kite's long line;
The day is done for girls and boys –
Look, it is almost nine!
Come, weary foot, and sleepy head,
Get up, and come along to bed.'

The children, loath, must yet obey;
Up the long stair they creep;
Lie down, and something sing or say
Until they fall asleep,
To steal through caverns of the night
Into the morning's golden light.

We, elder ones, sit up more late,
And tasks unfinished ply,
But, gently busy, watch and wait –
Dear sister, you and I,
To hear the Father, with soft tread,
Coming to carry us to bed.

George MacDonald

PRAISE OF WOMEN

No thyng ys to man so dere

As wommanys love in gode manere.

A gode womman is mannys blys,

There her love right and stedfast ys.

There ys no solas under hevene

Of alle that a man may nevene

That shulde a man so moche glew

As a gode womman that loveth true.

Ne derer is none in Goddis hurde

Than a chaste womman with lovely worde.

Robert Mannyng of Brunne

A FEW RULES FOR BEGINNERS

Babies must not eat the coal
And they must not make grimaces,
Nor in party dresses roll
And must never black their faces.

They must learn that pointing's rude,
They must sit quite still at table,
And must always eat the food
Put before them – if they're able.

If they fall, they must not cry,
Though it's known how painful this is;
No – there's always Mother by
Who will comfort them with kisses.

Katherine Mansfield

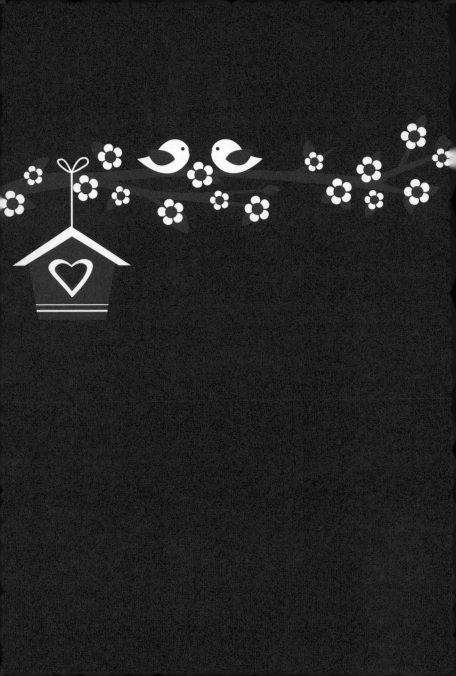

BUTTERFLY LAUGHTER

In the middle of our porridge plates
There was a blue butterfly painted
And each morning we tried who should reach the
butterfly first.
Then the Grandmother said: 'Do not eat the poor
butterfly.'
That made us laugh.
Always she said it and always it started us laughing.
It seemed such a sweet little joke.
I was certain that one fine morning
The butterfly would fly out of our plates,
Laughing the teeniest laugh in the world,
And perch on the Grandmother's lap.

Katherine Mansfield

FIRELIGHT

Playing in the fire and twilight together,
My little son and I,
Suddenly – woefully – I stoop to catch him.
'Try, mother, try!'

Old Nurse Silence lifts a silent finger:
'Hush! Cease your play!'
What happened? What in that tiny moment
Flew away?

Katherine Mansfield

TO A LITTLE CHILD

Clear eyes of heaven's chosen hue
When not a cloud is seen above
To fleck the warm untroubled blue,
A little laughing face of love;

A boundless energy of life
In dimpled arms and rosy feet;
No breath of care, no touch of strife,
Has dulled thy glad heart's rhythmic beat.

So girt about with golden light,
By shadows still so little vexed,
That many a weary anxious wight
Grows in thy presence less perplexed.

Our smiles come at thy fairy beck,
Frowns pass away at thy caress;
When thy soft arms are round my neck
I feel God's wondrous tenderness.

Annie Matheson

SLEEP

Soft silence of the summer night
Alive with wistful murmurings,
Enfold me in thy quiet might:
Shake o'er my head thy slumb'rous wings,
So cool and light:
Let me forget all earthly things
In sleep to-night!

Tired roses, passionately sweet,
Are leaning on their cool green leaves,
The mignonette about my feet
A maze of tangled fragrance weaves,
Where dewdrops meet:
Kind sleep the weary world bereaves
Of noise and heat.

White lilies, pure as falling snow,
And redolent of tenderness,
Are gently swaying to and fro,

Lulled by the breath of evening less
Than by the low
Music of sleepy winds, that bless
The buds that grow.

The air is like a mother's hand
Laid softly on a throbbing brow,
And o'er the darksome, dewy land
The peace of heaven is stealing now,
While, hand in hand,
Young angels tell the flowers how
Their lives are planned.

From yon deep sky the quiet stars
Look down with steadfast eloquence,
And God the prison-door unbars
That held the mute world's inmost sense
From all the wars
Of day's loud hurry and turbulence;
And nothing now the silence mars
Of love intense.

Annie Matheson

THE LADY OF THE LAMBS

She walks – the lady of my delight –
A shepherdess of sheep.
Her flocks are thoughts. She keeps them white;
She guards them from the steep.
She feeds them on the fragrant height,
And folds them in for sleep.

She roams maternal hills and bright,
Dark valleys safe and deep.
Her dreams are innocent at night;
The chastest stars may peep.
She walks – the lady of my delight –
A shepherdess of sheep.

She holds her little thoughts in sight,
Though gay they run and leap.
She is so circumspect and right;
She has her soul to keep.
She walks – the lady of my delight –
A shepherdess of sheep.

Alice Meynell

THE MODERN MOTHER

Oh what a kiss
With filial passion overcharged is this!
To this misgiving breast
The child runs, as a child ne'er ran to rest
Upon the light heart and the unoppressed.

Unhoped, unsought!
A little tenderness, this mother thought
The utmost of her meed
She looked for gratitude; content indeed
With thus much that her nine years' love had bought.

Nay, even with less.
This mother, giver of life, death, peace, distress,
Desired ah! not so much
Thanks as forgiveness; and the passing touch
Expected, and the slight, the brief caress.

O filial light

Strong in these childish eyes, these new, these bright

Intelligible stars! Their rays

Are near the constant earth, guides in the maze,

Natural, true, keen in this dusk of days.

Alice Meynell

MOTHERHOOD

The bravest battle that ever was fought!
Shall I tell you where and when?
On the maps of the world you will find it not;
'Twas fought by the mothers of men.
Nay not with the cannon of battle-shot,
With a sword or noble pen;
Nay, not with eloquent words or thought
From mouth of wonderful men!
But deep in a walled-up woman's heart –
Of a woman that would not yield,
But bravely, silently bore her part –
Lo, there is the battlefield!
No marshalling troops, no bivouac song,
No banner to gleam and wave;
But oh! those battles, they last so long –
From babyhood to the grave.
Yet, faithful still as a bridge of stars,
She fights in her walled-up town –
Fights on and on in her endless wars,
Then silent, unseen, goes down.

Oh, ye with banners and battle-shot,
  And soldiers to shout and praise!
I tell you the kingliest victories fought
  Were fought in those silent ways.
O spotless woman in a world of shame,
  With splendid and silent scorn,
Go back to God as white as you came –
  The Kingliest warrior born!

Joaquin Miller

TO MY MOTHER SLEEPING

Sleep on, my mother! sweet and innocent dreams
Attend thee, best and dearest! Dreams that gild
Life's clouds like setting suns, with pleasures filled
And saintly joy, such as thy mind beseems,
Thy mind where never stormy passion gleams,
Where their soft nest the dove-like virtues build;
And calmest thoughts, like violets distilled,
Their fragrance mingle with bright wisdom's beams.

Sleep on, my mother! not the lily's bell
So sweet; not the enamoured west-wind's sighs
That shake the dew-drop from her snowy cell
So gentle; not that dew-drop ere it flies
So pure. Even slumber loves with thee to dwell,
O model most beloved of good and wise.

Mary Russell Mitford

DOWN HOME

Down home to-night the moonshine falls
Across a hill with daisies pied,
The pear tree by the garden gate
Beckons with white arms like a bride.

A savor as of trampled fern
Along the whispering meadow stirs,
And, beacon of immortal love,
A light is shining through the firs.

To my old gable window creeps
The night wind with a sigh and song,
And, weaving ancient sorceries,
Thereto the gleeful moonbeams throng

Beside the open kitchen door
My mother stands all lovingly,
And o'er the pathways of the dark
She sends a yearning thought to me.

It seeks and finds my answering heart
Which shall no more be peace-possessed
Until I reach her empty arms
And lay my head upon her breast.

Lucy Maud Montgomery

THE MOTHER

Here I lean over you, small son, sleeping
Warm in my arms,
And I con to my heart all your dew-fresh charms,
As you lie close, close in my hungry hold…
Your hair like a miser's dream of gold,
And the white rose of your face far fairer,
Finer, and rarer
Than all the flowers in the young year's keeping;
Over lips half parted your low breath creeping
Is sweeter than violets in April grasses;
Though your eyes are fast shut I can see their blue,
Splendid and soft as starshine in heaven,
With all the joyance and wisdom given
From the many souls who have stanchly striven
Through the dead years to be strong and true.

Those fine little feet in my worn hands holden…
Where will they tread?
Valleys of shadow or heights dawn-red?
And those silken fingers, O, wee, white son,

What valorous deeds shall by them be done

In the future that yet so distant is seeming

To my fond dreaming?

What words all so musical and golden

With starry truth and poesy olden

Shall those lips speak in the years on-coming?

O, child of mine, with waxen brow,

Surely your words of that dim to-morrow

Rapture and power and grace must borrow

From the poignant love and holy sorrow

Of the heart that shrines and cradles you now!

Some bitter day you will love another,

To her will bear

Love-gifts and woo her... then must I share

You and your tenderness! Now you are mine

From your feet to your hair so golden and fine,

And your crumpled finger-tips... mine completely,

Wholly and sweetly;

Mine with kisses deep to smother,

No one so near to you now as your mother!

Others may hear your words of beauty,

But your precious silence is mine alone;
Here in my arms I have enrolled you,
Away from the grasping world I fold you,
Flesh of my flesh and bone of my bone!

Lucy Maud Montgomery

TO MY MOTHER

They tell us of an Indian tree
Which howsoe'er the sun and sky
May tempt its boughs to wander free,
And shoot and blossom, wide and high,
Far better loves to bend its arms
Downward again to that dear earth
From which the life that fills and warms
Its grateful being, first had birth,
'Tis thus, though wooed by flattering friends,
And fed with fame (if fame it may be),
This heart, my own dear mother, bends,
With love's true instinct, back to thee!

Thomas Moore

FROM MOTHER AND SON

Now sleeps the land of houses, and dead night holds the street,

And there thou liest, my baby, and sleepest soft and sweet;

My man is away for awhile, but safe and alone we lie;

And none heareth thy breath but thy mother, and the moon looking

down from the sky

On the weary waste of the town, as it looked on the grass-edged road

Still warm with yesterday's sun, when I left my old abode,

Hand in hand with my love, that night of all nights in the year;

When the river of love o'erflowed and drowned all doubt and fear,

And we two were alone in the world, and once, if never again,

We knew of the secret of earth and the tale of its labour and pain.

William Morris

FROM THE ITALIAN

As a little child whom his mother has chidden,
Wrecked in the dark in a storm of weeping,
Sleeps with his tear-stained eyes closed hidden
And, with fists clenched, sobs still in his sleeping,

So in my breast sleeps Love, O white lady,
What does he care though the rest are playing,
With rattles and drums in the woodlands shady,
Happy children, whom Joy takes maying!

Ah, do not wake him, lest you should hear him
Scolding the others, breaking their rattles,
Smashing their drums, when their play comes near him –
Love who, for me, is a god of battles!

Edith Nesbit

FROM THE TUSCAN

When in the west the red sun sank in glory,
The cypress trees stood up like gold, fine gold;
The mother told her little child the story
Of the gold trees the heavenly gardens hold.

In golden dreams the child sees golden rivers,
Gold trees, gold blossoms, golden boughs and leaves,
Without, the cypress in the night wind shivers,
Weeps with the rain and with the darkness grieves.

Edith Nesbit

FROM THE MOAT HOUSE

Oh, baby, baby, baby dear,
We lie alone together here;
The snowy gown and cap and sheet
With lavender are fresh and sweet;
Through half-closed blinds the roses peer
To see and love you, baby dear.

We are so tired, we like to lie
Just doing nothing, you and I,
Within the darkened quiet room.
The sun sends dusk rays through the gloom,
Which is no gloom since you are here,
My little life, my baby dear.

Soft sleepy mouth so vaguely pressed
Against your new-made mother's breast,
Soft little hands in mine I fold,
Soft little feet I kiss and hold,
Round soft smooth head and tiny ear,
All mine, my own, my baby dear.

And he we love is far away!
But he will come some happy day.
You need but me, and I can rest
At peace with you beside me pressed.
There are no questions, longings vain,
No murmuring, nor doubt, nor pain,
Only content and we are here,
My baby dear.

Edith Nesbit

ON SEEING HER TWO SONS AT PLAY

Sweet age of blest delusion! blooming boys,

Ah! revel long in childhood's thoughtless joys,

With light and pliant spirits, that can stoop

To follow sportively the rolling hoop;

To watch the sleeping top with gay delight,

Or mark with raptur'd gaze the sailing kite;

Or eagerly pursuing Pleasure's call,

Can find it centr'd in the bounding ball!

Alas! the day *will* come, when sports like these

Must lose their magic, and their power to please;

Too swiftly fled, the rosy hours of youth

Shall yield their fairy-charms to mournful Truth;

Even now, a mother's fond prophetic fear

Sees the dark train of human ills appear;

Views various fortune for each lovely child,

Storms for the bold, and anguish for the mild;

Beholds already those expressive eyes

Beam a sad certainty of future sighs;

And dreads each suffering those dear breasts may know
In their long passage through a world of woe;
Perchance predestin'd every pang to prove,
That treacherous friends inflict, or faithless love;
For ah! how few have found existence sweet,
Where grief is sure, but happiness deceit!

Lady Henrietta O'Neil

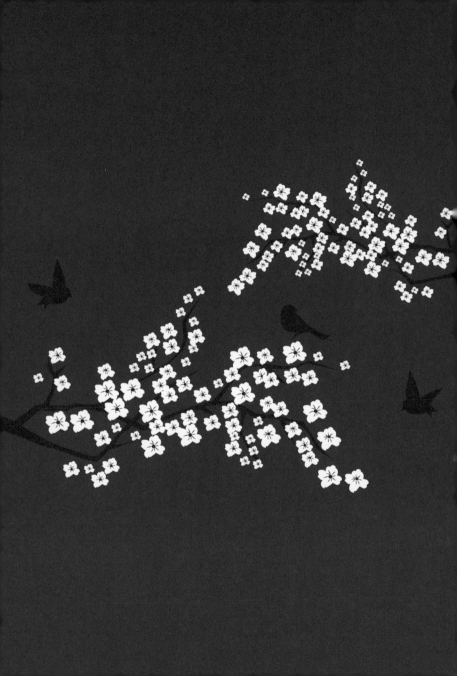

TO MY MOTHER

Because I feel that, in the Heavens above,
The angels, whispering to one another,
Can find, among their burning terms of love,
None so devotional as that of 'Mother',
Therefore by that dear name I long have called you –
You who are more than mother unto me,
And fill my heart of hearts, where Death installed you
In setting my Virginia's spirit free.
My mother – my own mother, who died early,
Was but the mother of myself; but you
Are mother to the one I loved so dearly,
And thus are dearer than the mother I knew
By that infinity with which my wife
Was dearer to my soul than its soul-life.

Edgar Allan Poe

FROM PROVERBS
(31: 10, 25-31)

Who can find a virtuous woman?

for her price is far above rubies.

[…]

Strength and honour are her clothing;

and she shall rejoice in time to come.

She openeth her mouth with wisdom;

and in her tongue is the law of kindness.

She looketh well to the ways of her household,

and eateth not the bread of idleness.

Her children arise up, and call her blessed;

her husband also, and he praiseth her.

Many daughters have done virtuously,

but thou excellest them all.

Favour is deceitful, and beauty is vain:

but a woman that feareth the Lord, she shall be praised.

Give her the fruit of her hands;

and let her own works praise her in the gates.

HOLY INNOCENTS

Sleep, little Baby, sleep;
The holy Angels love thee,
And guard thy bed, and keep
A blessed watch above thee.
No spirit can come near
Nor evil beast to harm thee:
Sleep, Sweet, devoid of fear
Where nothing need alarm thee.

The Love which doth not sleep,
The eternal arms surround thee:
The shepherd of the sheep
In perfect love hath found thee.
Sleep through the holy night,
Christ-kept from snare and sorrow,
Until thou wake to light
And love and warmth to-morrow.

Christina Rossetti

SONNETS ARE FULL OF LOVE

Sonnets are full of love, and this my tome
Has many sonnets: so here now shall be
One sonnet more, a love sonnet, from me
To her whose heart is my heart's quiet home,
To my first Love, my Mother, on whose knee
I learnt love-lore that is not troublesome;
Whose service is my special dignity,
And she my loadstar while I go and come
And so because you love me, and because
I love you, Mother, I have woven a wreath
Of rhymes wherewith to crown your honored name:
In you not fourscore years can dim the flame
Of love, whose blessed glow transcends the laws
Of time and change and mortal life and death.

Christina Rossetti

BRIDAL SONG

Roses, their sharp spines being gone,
Not royal in their smells alone,
But in their hue;
Maiden pinks, of odour faint,
Daisies smell-less, yet most quaint,
And sweet thyme true;

Primrose, firstborn child of Ver;
Merry springtime's harbinger,
With her bells dim;
Oxlips in their cradles growing,
Marigolds on death-beds blowing,
Larks'-heels trim;

All dear Nature's children sweet
Lie 'fore bride and bridegroom's feet,
Blessing their sense!
Not an angel of the air,
Bird melodious or bird fair,
Be absent hence!

The crow, the slanderous cuckoo, nor
The boding raven, nor chough hoar,
Nor chattering pye,
May on our bride-house perch or sing,
Or with them any discord bring,
But from it fly!

William Shakespeare

THE CHILD'S QUEST

My mother twines me roses wet with dew;
Oft have I sought the garden through and through;
I cannot find the tree whereon
My mother's roses grew.
Seek not, O child, the tree whereon
Thy mother's roses grew.

My mother tells me tales of noble deeds;
Oft have I sought her book when no one heeds;
I cannot find the page, alas,
From which my mother reads.
Seek not, O child, to find the page
From which thy mother reads.

My mother croons me songs all soft and low,
Through the white night where little breezes blow;
Yet never when the morning dawns,
My mother's songs I know.
Seek not, O child, at dawn of day
Thy mother's songs to know.

Frances Shaw

COME, MY LITTLE CHILDREN, HERE ARE SONGS FOR YOU

Come, my little children, here are songs for you;

Some are short and some are long, and all, all are new.

You must learn to sing them very small and clear,

Very true to time and tune and pleasing to the ear.

Mark the note that rises, mark the notes that fall,

Mark the time when broken, and the swing of it all.

So when night is come, and you have gone to bed,

All the songs you love to sing shall echo in your head.

Robert Louis Stevenson

MY WIFE

Trusty, dusky, vivid, true,
With eyes of gold and bramble-dew,
Steel-true and blade-straight,
The great artificer
Made my mate.

Honour, anger, valour, fire;
A love that life could never tire,
Death quench or evil stir,
The mighty master
Gave to her.

Teacher, tender, comrade, wife,
A fellow-farer true through life,
Heart-whole and soul-free
The august father
Gave to me.

Robert Louis Stevenson

THE SICK CHILD

Child. O mother, lay your hand on my brow!
O mother, mother, where am I now?
Why is the room so gaunt and great?
Why am I lying awake so late?

Mother. Fear not at all: the night is still.
Nothing is here that means you ill –
Nothing but lamps the whole town through,
And never a child awake but you.

Child. Mother, mother, speak low in my ear,
Some of the things are so great and near,
Some are so small and far away,
I have a fear that I cannot stay.
What have I done, and what do I fear,
And why are you crying, mother dear?

Mother. Out in the city, sounds begin
Thank the kind God, the carts come in!
An hour or two more and God is so kind,

The day shall be blue in the windowblind,
Then shall my child go sweetly asleep,
And dream of the birds and the hills of sheep.

Robert Louis Stevenson

TO MY MOTHER

You too, my mother, read my rhymes
For love of unforgotten times,
And you may chance to hear once more
The little feet along the floor.

Robert Louis Stevenson

YOUNG NIGHT THOUGHT

All night long and every night,
When my mama puts out the light,
I see the people marching by,
As plain as day, before my eye.

Armies and emperors and kings,
All carrying different kinds of things,
And marching in so grand a way,
You never saw the like by day.

So fine a show was never seen
At the great circus on the green;
For every kind of beast and man
Is marching in that caravan.

At first they move a little slow,
But still the faster on they go,
And still beside them close I keep
Until we reach the town of Sleep.

Robert Louis Stevenson

THE SWING

How do you like to go up in a swing,
Up in the air so blue?
Oh, I do think it the pleasantest thing
Ever a child can do!

Up in the air and over the wall,
Till I can see so wide,
River and trees and cattle and all
Over the countryside –

Till I look down on the garden green,
Down on the roof so brown –
Up in the air I go flying again,
Up in the air and down!

Robert Louis Stevenson

FIRST FOOTSTEPS

A little way, more soft and sweet
Than fields aflower with May,
A babe's feet, venturing, scarce complete
A little way.

Eyes full of dawning day
Look up for mother's eyes to meet,
Too blithe for song to say.

Glad as the golden spring to greet
Its first live leaflet's play.
Love, laughing, leads the little feet
A little way.

Algernon Charles Swinburne

THE WASHING AND DRESSING

Ah! why will my dear little girl be so cross,
And cry, and look sulky, and pout?
To lose her sweet smile is a terrible loss,
I can't even kiss her without.

You say you don't like to be wash'd and be dress'd,
But would you not wish to be clean?
Come, drive that long sob from your dear little breast,
This face is not fit to be seen.

If the water is cold, and the brush hurts your head,
And the soap has got into your eye,
Will the water grow warmer for all that you've said?
And what good will it do you to cry?

It is not to tease you and hurt you, my sweet,
But only for kindness and care,
That I wash you, and dress you, and make you look neat,
And comb out your tanglesome hair.

I don't mind the trouble, if you would not cry,
But pay me for all with a kiss;
That's right – take the towel and wipe your wet eye,
I thought you'd be good after this.

Ann Taylor

THE BABY'S DANCE

Dance little baby, dance up high,
Never mind baby, mother is by;
Crow and caper, caper and crow,
There little baby, there you go;
Up to the ceiling, down to the ground,
Backwards and forwards, round and round;
Dance little baby, and mother shall sing,
With the merry coral, ding, ding, ding.

Ann Taylor

FROM THE PRINCESS

I loved her, one
Not learned, save in gracious household ways,
Nor perfect, nay, but full of tender wants,
No angel, but a dearer being, all dipt
In angel instincts, breathing Paradise,
Interpreter between the gods and men,
Who looked all native to her place, and yet
On tiptoe seem'd to touch upon a sphere
Too gross to tread, and all male minds perforce
Swayed to her from their orbits as they moved,
And girdled her with music. Happy he
With such a mother! faith in womankind
Beats with his blood, and trust in all things high
Comes easy to him, and tho' he trip and fall,
He shall not blind his soul with clay.

Alfred Tennyson

SWEET AND LOW

Sweet and low, sweet and low,
Wind of the western sea,
Low, low, breathe and blow,
Wind of the western sea!
Over the rolling waters go,
Come from the dying moon, and blow,
Blow him again to me;
While my little one, while my pretty one, sleeps.

Sleep and rest, sleep and rest,
Father will come to thee soon;
Rest, rest, on mother's breast,
Father will come to thee soon;
Father will come to his babe in the nest;
Silver sails all out of the west
Under the silver moon:
Sleep, my little one, sleep, my pretty one, sleep.

Alfred Tennyson

A WISH

'Be my fairy, mother,
Give me a wish a day;
Something as well as sunshine,
As when the rain-drops play.'

'And if I were a fairy,
With but one wish to spare,
What should I give thee, darling,
To quiet thine earnest prayer?'

'I'd like a little brook, mother,
All for my very own,
To laugh all day among the trees,
And shine on the mossy stone;

'To run right under the window,
And sing me fast asleep;
With soft steps and a tender sound,
Over the grass to creep.

'Make it run down the hill, mother,
With a leap like a tinkling bell,
So fast I never can catch the leaf
That into its fountain fell.

'Make it as wild as a frightened bird.
As crazy as a bee,
With a noise like the baby's funny laugh –
That's the brook for me!'

Rose Terry Cooke

FROM MOTHER'S DAY PROCLAMATION

Arise then... women of this day!

Arise, all women who have hearts,

Whether your baptism be of water or of tears!

Say firmly:

'We will not have questions decided by irrelevant agencies,

Our husbands will not come to us, reeking with carnage,

For caresses and applause.

Our sons shall not be taken from us to unlearn

All that we have been able to teach them of charity, mercy

and patience.

We, the women of one country,

Will be too tender of those of another country

To allow our sons to be trained to injure theirs.'

Julia Ward Howe

FROM CRADLE HYMN

Hush, my dear, lie still and slumber,
Holy angels guard thy bed;
Heavenly blessings, without number,
Gently falling on thy head.

How much better thou art attended
Than the Son of God could be,
When from heaven He descended,
And became a child like thee!

Soft and easy is thy cradle;
Coarse and hard thy Saviour lay,
When His birthplace was a stable,
And His softest bed was hay.

I could give thee thousand kisses,
Hoping what I most desire;
Not a mother's fondest wishes
Can to greater joys aspire.

May'st thou live to know and fear Him,
Trust and love Him all thy days;
Then go dwell forever near Him,
See His face, and sing His praise!

Isaac Watts

CHOOSING

The thrush that, yet alone, pipes for his mate
Knows she will come in time to build the nest,
Knows she'll be she his tiny soul loves best;
'Tis love-time at the hawthorn blossom's date:
And the new flower-cups bare their hearts and wait
While careless breezes bring them love for guest;
And Youth laughs ready for the glad unrest;
But Love that chooses lingers desolate.

And I, who seek, and yearn for love to stir,
And I, who seek, and cannot love but one
And have not known her being, nor can find,
I take my homeless way for sake of her;
And love-time's here, and love-time will be done:
Birds end all singing in the autumn wind.

Augusta Webster

BEAUTIFUL WOMEN

Women sit, or move to and fro – some old, some young;
The young are beautiful – but the old are more beautiful
than the young.

Walt Whitman

FROM OUT OF THE CRADLE ENDLESSLY ROCKING

Out of the cradle endlessly rocking,

Out of the mocking-bird's throat, the musical shuttle,

Out of the Ninth-month midnight,

Over the sterile sands, and the fields beyond, where the child, leaving

his bed, wander'd alone, bare-headed, barefoot,

Down from the shower'd halo,

Up from the mystic play of shadows, twining and twisting as if

they were alive,

Out from the patches of briers and blackberries,

From the memories of the bird that chanted to me,

From your memories, sad brother – from the fitful risings and

fallings I heard,

From under that yellow half-moon, late-risen, and swollen as if

with tears,

From those beginning notes of sickness and love, there in the

transparent mist,

From the thousand responses of my heart, never to cease,

From the myriad thence-arous'd words,

From the word stronger and more delicious than any,

From such, as now they start, the scene revisiting,

As a flock, twittering, rising, or overhead passing,

Borne hither – ere all eludes me, hurriedly,

A man – yet by these tears a little boy again,

Throwing myself on the sand, confronting the waves,

I, chanter of pains and joys, uniter of here and hereafter,

Taking all hints to use them – but swiftly leaping beyond them,

A reminiscence sing.

Walt Whitman

MOTHER AND BABE

I see the sleeping babe, nestling the breast of its mother;
The sleeping mother and babe – hush'd, I study them long and long.

Walt Whitman

FROM THERE WAS A CHILD WENT FORTH

There was a child went forth every day;

And the first object he look'd upon, that object he became;

And that object became part of him for the day, or a certain part of

the day, or for many years, or stretching cycles of years.

The early lilacs became part of this child,

And grass, and white and red morning-glories, and white and red

clover, and the song of the phoebe-bird,

And the Third-month lambs, and the sow's pink-faint litter, and the

mare's foal, and the cow's calf,

And the noisy brood of the barn-yard, or by the mire

of the pond-side,

And the fish suspending themselves so curiously below there –

and the beautiful curious liquid,

And the water-plants with their graceful flat heads – all became

part of him.

The field-sprouts of Fourth-month and Fifth-month became

part of him;

Winter-grain sprouts, and those of the light-yellow corn, and the esculent roots of the garden,

And the apple-trees cover'd with blossoms, and the fruit afterward, and wood-berries, and the commonest weeds by the road;

And the old drunkard staggering home from the out-house of the tavern, whence he had lately risen,

And the school-mistress that pass'd on her way to the school,

And the friendly boys that pass'd – and the quarrelsome boys,

And the tidy and fresh-cheek'd girls – and the barefoot negro boy and girl,

And all the changes of city and country, wherever he went.

His own parents,

He that had father'd him, and she that had conceiv'd him in her womb, and birth'd him,

They gave this child more of themselves than that;

They gave him afterward every day – they became part of him.

Walt Whitman

A BABY IN THE HOUSE

I knew that a baby was hid in that house,
Though I saw no cradle and heard no cry;
But the husband was tip-toeing 'round like a mouse,
And the good wife was humming a soft lullaby;
And there was a look on the face of the mother,
That I knew could mean only one thing, and no other.

The mother, I said to myself, for I knew
That the woman before me was certainly that;
And there lay in a corner a tiny cloth shoe,
And I saw on a stand such a wee little hat;
And the beard of the husband said, plain as could be,
'Two fat chubby hands have been tugging at me.'

And he took from his pocket a gay picture-book,
And a dog that could bark, if you pulled on a string;
And the wife laid them up with such a pleased look;
And I said to myself, 'There is no other thing
But a babe that could bring about all this, and so
That one thing is in hiding somewhere, I know.'

I stayed but a moment, and saw nothing more,
And heard not a sound, yet I know I was right;
What else could the shoe mean that lay on the floor,
The book and the toy, and the faces so bright;
And what made the husband as still as a mouse?
I am sure, very sure, there's a babe in that house.

Ella Wheeler Wilcox

BABY'S FIRST JOURNEY

Lightly they hold him and lightly they sway him –
Soft as a pillow are somebody's arms.
Down he goes slowly, ever so lowly
Over the rim of the cradle they lay him –
Baby's first journey is free from alarms.

Baby is growing while Mama sings by-lo,
Sturdy and rosy and laughing and fair,
Crowing and growing past every one's knowing,
Out goes the cradle and in comes the 'high-lo',
Baby's next journey is into this chair.

Crying or cooing or waking or sleeping,
Baby is ever a thing to adore.
Look at him yonder – oh what a wonder,
Who would believe it, the darling is creeping,
Baby's next journey is over the floor.

Sweeter and cuter and brighter and stronger,
Mama can see every day how he's grown.

Shoes are all battered, stockings all tattered,

Oh! but the baby is baby no longer

Look at the fellow – he's walking alone!

Ella Wheeler Wilcox

THE CHILD LEANS ON ITS PARENT'S BREAST

The child leans on its parent's breast,
Leaves there its cares, and is at rest;
The bird sits singing by his nest,
And tells aloud
His trust in God, and so is blest
'Neath every cloud.

He has no store, he sows no seed,
Yet sings aloud, and doth not heed;
By flowing stream or grassy mead
He sings to shame
Men, who forget, in fear of need,
A Father's name.

The heart that trusts for ever sings,
And feels as light as it had wings;
A well of peace within it springs;

Come good or ill,
Whate'er to-day, to-morrow brings,
It is His will!

Isaac Williams

MY GRANDCHILDREN AT CHURCH

Bright Dorothy, with eyes of blue,
And serious Dickie, brave as fair,
Crossing to Church you oft may view
When no one but myself is there:
First to the belfry they repair,
And, while to the long ropes they cling,
And make believe to call to prayer,
For angels' ears the bells they ring.

Next, seated gravely in a pew
A pulpit homily they share,
Meet for my little flock of two,
Pointed and plain, as they can bear:
Then venture up the pulpit stair,
Pray at the desk or gaily sing:
O sweet child-life, without a care –
For angels' ears the bells they ring.

Dear little ones, the early dew
Of holy infancy they wear,
And lift to Heaven a face as true
As flowers that breathe the morning air
Whate'er they do, where'er they fare,
They can command an angel's wing:
Their voices have a music rare, –
For angels' ears the bells they ring.

O parents, of your charge beware;
Their angels stand before the King;
In work, play, sleep, and everywhere
For angels' ears the bells they ring.

Richard Wilton

FROM ODE: INTIMATIONS OF IMMORTALITY FROM RECOLLECTIONS OF EARLY CHILDHOOD

Behold the Child among his new-born blisses,
A six years' darling of a pigmy size!
See, where 'mid work of his own hand he lies,
Fretted by sallies of his mother's kisses,
With light upon him from his father's eyes!
See, at his feet, some little plan or chart,
Some fragment from his dream of human life,
Shaped by himself with newly-learned art;
A wedding or a festival,
A mourning or a funeral;
And this hath now his heart,
And unto this he frames his song:
Then will he fit his tongue
To dialogues of business, love, or strife;
But it will not be long

Ere this be thrown aside,

And with new joy and pride

The little actor cons another part;

Filling from time to time his 'humorous stage'

With all the Persons, down to palsied Age,

That Life brings with her in her equipage;

As if his whole vocation

Were endless imitation.

William Wordsworth

FROM THE EMIGRANT MOTHER

Dear Babe, thou daughter of another,
One moment let me be thy mother!
An infant's face and looks are thine,
And sure a mother's heart is mine:
Thy own dear mother's far away,
At labour in the harvest field:
Thy little sister is at play; –
What warmth, what comfort would it yield
To my poor heart, if thou wouldst be
One little hour a child to me!

William Wordsworth

FROM PERFECT WOMAN

She was a phantom of delight
When first she gleam'd upon my sight;
A lovely apparition, sent
To be a moment's ornament;
Her eyes as stars of twilight fair;
Like twilight's, too, her dusky hair;
But all things else about her drawn
From May-time and the cheerful dawn;
A dancing shape, an image gay,
To haunt, to startle, and waylay.

I saw her upon nearer view,
A Spirit, yet a Woman too!
Her household motions light and free,
And steps of virgin liberty;
A countenance in which did meet
Sweet records, promises as sweet;
A creature not too bright or good
For human nature's daily food;
For transient sorrows, simple wiles,
Praise, blame, love, kisses, tears, and smiles.

William Wordsworth

LOVE, A CHILD,
IS EVER CRYING

Love, a child, is ever crying;
Please him, and he straight is flying;
Give him, he the more is craving,
Never satisfied with having.

His desires have no measure;
Endless folly is his treasure;
What he promiseth he breaketh;
Trust not one word that he speaketh.

He vows nothing but false matter;
And to cozen you will flatter;
Let him gain the hand, he'll leave you
And still glory to deceive you.

He will triumph in your wailing;
And yet cause be of your failing:
These his virtues are, and slighter
Are his gifts, his favours lighter.

Feathers are as firm in staying;
Wolves no fiercer in their preying;
As a child then, leave him crying;
Nor seek him so given to flying.

Lady Mary Wroth

THE PLAYER QUEEN

My mother dandled me and sang,
'How young it is, how young!'
And made a golden cradle
That on a willow swung.

'He went away,' my mother sang,
'When I was brought to bed,'
And all the while her needle pulled
The gold and silver thread.

She pulled the thread and bit the thread
And made a golden gown,
And wept because she dreamt that I
Was born to wear a crown.

'When she was got,' my mother sang,
'I heard a sea-mew cry,
And saw a flake of the yellow foam
That dropped upon my thigh.'

How therefore could she help but braid
The gold into my hair,
And dream that I should carry
The golden top of care?

William Butler Yeats

FROM A PRAYER FOR MY DAUGHTER

In courtesy I'd have her chiefly learned;
Hearts are not had as a gift but hearts are earned
By those that are not entirely beautiful;
Yet many, that have played the fool
For beauty's very self, has charm made wise.
And many a poor man that has roved,
Loved and thought himself beloved,
From a glad kindness cannot take his eyes.

May she become a flourishing hidden tree
That all her thoughts may like the linnet be,
And have no business but dispensing round
Their magnanimities of sound,
Nor but in merriment begin a chase,
Nor but in merriment a quarrel.
O may she live like some green laurel
Rooted in one dear perpetual place.

William Butler Yeats

www.summersdale.com